SEIKO 74A

ENGLAND
WALES

Wednesday...

Wembley
OFFICIAL SOUVENIR PROGRAMME 60p

Wembley Stadium
Official programme 50p

ENGLAND
GERMANY
CHARLEROI
JUNE, 17

FOOTBALL ASSOCIATION INTERNATIONAL

RITISH CHAMPIONSHIP
Wembley Stadium
Wednesday 20th May, 1981. Kick-Off 7.45pm.

ENGLAND v WALES
Official Programme 50p

EUROPEAN CHAMP
v Denmark

Wednesday 21st September 1983
Kick-Off 7-45pm
Wembley Stadium
Official Souvenir Programme 60p

UEFA

FRANCE v
NETHERLANDS
Saturday 22nd June
Anfield · Kick-off 6.30pm

ENGLAND v SPAIN
Saturday 22nd June
Wembley · Kick-off 3.00pm

UEFA EUROPEAN FOOTBALL CHAMPIONSHIP · 8th-30th JUNE 1996

SEMI-FINALS
OFFICIAL MATCHDAY
PROGRAMME £4.00

Euro 96
England

Free Lions
THE ENGLAND FANZINE FROM THE FOOTBALL SUPPORTERS' FEDERATION

ISSUE 5

FSF
THE FOOTBALL SUPPORTERS' FEDERATION

21

SWEDEN v ENGLAND 20TH JUNE 2006

SUPPORTED BY
Nationwide PRIDE. PASSION. BELIEF.

UEF

VM-
kvalifisering

Ulleval Stadion

ORGE—ENGLAND

ag 9. september 1981 kl. 19.00. Pris kr. 5,-

KREDITKASSEN
- bank for folk flest

OFFICIAL
PROGRAMME
The 1986 FIFA World Cup
U.K. Edition
£2.00

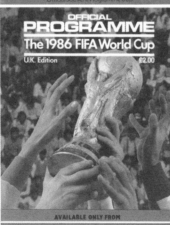

AVAILABLE ONLY FROM

FRANCE v
CZECH REP.
GERMANY v
ENGLAND

UEFA

FRANCE v CZECH REP.
Wednesday 26th June
Old Trafford · Kick-off 4.00pm

GERMANY v ENGLAND
Wednesday 26th June
Wembley · Kick-off 7.30pm

UEFA EUROPEAN FOOTBALL CHAMPIONSHIP · 8th-30th JUNE 1996

Free Lions
THE ENGLAND FANZINE FROM THE FOOTBALL SUPPORTERS' FEDERATION

ISSUE 6

FSF
THE FOOTBALL SUPPORTERS' FEDERATION

16

ENGLAND v PORTUGAL, 1ST JULY 2006

SUPPORTED BY
Nationwide PRIDE. PASSION. BELIEF.

OPEAN CHAMPIONSHIP FOOTBALL

British Championship
ENGLAND
v
NORTHERN IRELAND

PROGRAMME OFFICIEL

COUPE DU MONDE

FRANCE 98
COUPE DU MONDE

8PM FRIDAY 1 JUNE 2007 WEMBLEY STADIUM £5
ENGLAND
v BRAZIL

"I'VE BEEN
DREAMING

THREE
LIONS

For my wife, Bozenka, and my children, Jenny, Ben and Sam
and to the memory of my father, Gerald, my mother, Vera,
and my sister Lorraine. I know they would be as proud of it as
I am. Finally, this book is sincerely dedicated to the millions of
England supporters who, like me, have waited in vain for
something to go alongside the Jules Rimet Trophy other
than the FIFA Fair Play Trophy.

First published in Great Britain in 2007 by Atlantic Books,
an imprint of Grove Atlantic Ltd.

1 2 3 4 5 6 7 8 9

A CIP catalogue record for this book is available from the
British Library.

Hardback ISBN: 978 1 84354 662 7
Trade Paperback ISBN: 978 1 84354 663 4

Produced by Essential Works
www.essentialworks.co.uk
Editor: Mal Peachey
Designer: Kate Ward

Atlantic Books
An imprint of Grove Atlantic Ltd
Ormond House
26–27 Boswell Street
London WC1N 3JZ

Printed in Singapore

THREE LIONS

THE *unofficial* STORY OF THE
ENGLAND FOOTBALL TEAM SINCE 1966

BRIAN BEARD

Atlantic Books

London

CONTENTS

ENGLAND V BRAZIL (POST-30 JULY 1966)

THE GAMES

Brazil 2 [Goncalves, Ventura] v England 1 [Bell]

12 June 1969 (Maracana, Brazil) Friendly

England 0 v Brazil 1 [Jairzinho]

7 June 1970 (Guadalajara, Mexico) World Cup Group C

Brazil 1 [de Oliveira] v England 0

23 May 1976 (Los Angeles, USA) US Bi-Centennial
Tournament

Brazil 0 v England 0

8 June 1977 (Maracana, Brazil) Friendly

England 1 [Keegan] v Brazil 1 [Alves]

19 April 1978 (Wembley) Friendly

England 0 v Brazil 1 [Antunes]

12 July 1981 (Wembley) Friendly

Brazil 0 v England 2 [Barnes J, Hateley]

10 June 1984 (Maracana, Brazil) Friendly

England 1 [Lineker] v Brazil 1 [Lima]

19 May 1987 (Wembley) Rous Cup

England 1 [Lineker] v Brazil 0

28 Mar 1990 (Wembley) Friendly

England 1 [Platt] v Brazil 1 [de Gama]

17 May 1992 (Wembley) Friendly

England 1 [Platt] v Brazil 1 [Santos]

13 June 1993 (Washington DC, USA) US Cup

England 1 [Le Saux] v Brazil 3 [Junior, de Lima, Alves]

11 June 1995 (Wembley) Umbro Int. Tournament

England 0 v Brazil 1 [de Souza]

10 June 1997 (Paris, France) Tournoi de France

England 1 [Owen] v Brazil 1 [Sena]

27 May 2000 (Wembley) Friendly

England 1 [Owen] v Brazil 2 [Rivaldo, Ronaldinho]

21 June 2002 (Shizuoka, Japan) World Cup quarter-final

England 1 [Terry] v Brazil 1 [Diego]

1 June 2007 (Wembley) Friendly

ENGLAND V GERMANY (POST-30 JULY 1966)

THE GAMES

W Germany 1 [Beckenbauer] v England 0

1 June 1968 (Hanover, West Germany) Friendly

W Germany 3 [Beckenbauer, Seeler, Muller] v England 2
[Mullery, Peters]

14 June 1970 (Leon, Mexico) World Cup quarter-final

England 1 [Lee] v W Germany 3 [Hoeness, Netzer (pen), Muller]

29 April 1972 (Wembley) Euro qualifier

W Germany 0 v England 0

13 May 1972 (Berlin, East Germany) Euro qualifier

England 2 [Bell, MacDonald] v W Germany 0

12 Mar 1975 (Wembley) Friendly

W Germany 2 [Worm, Bonhoff] v England 1 [Pearson]

22 Feb 1978 (Munich, West Germany)

W Germany 0 v England 0

29 June 1982 (Madrid, Spain) World Cup 2nd round

England 1 [Woodcock] v W Germany 2 [Rummenigge 2]

13 Oct 1982 (Wembley) Friendly

England 3 [Dixon K (2), Robson] v W Germany 0

12 June 1985 (Mexico City, Mexico) Azteca 2000 Tournament

W Germany 3 [Litbarski (2), Wuttke] v England 1 [Lineker]

9 Sept 1987 (Dusseldorf, West Germany) Friendly

W Germany 1 [Brehme] v England 1 [Lineker] *4-3 pen, AET

4 July 1990 (Turin, Italy) World Cup semi-final

England 0 v Germany 1 [Riedle]

11 Sept 1991 (Wembley) Friendly

England 1 [Shearer] v Germany 1 [Kuntz] *5-6 pen, AET

26 June 1996 (Wembley) Euro Championships semi-final

England 1 [Shearer] v Germany 0

20 June 2000 (Charleroi, France) Euro Championships Group A

England 0 v Germany 1 [Hamman]

7 Oct 2000 (Wembley) World Cup qualifier

Germany 1 [Jancker] v England 5 [Owen (3), Gerrard, Heskey]

1 Sept 2001 (Munich, Germany) World Cup qualifier

'A HOLLOW, TAWDRY VICTORY' (*DAILY MIRROR*)

Revie's men might have beaten the Finns, but the inability to improve goal difference against a team of part-timers was to prove crucial and everyone except the manager seemed to know it. *The Times* called it 'a laborious, ineffective and insulting' win. Not for the first time since 1966, a technically superior set of players embarrassed England. And they were amateurs.

As Revie celebrated his second anniversary in charge he had to delay team selection for the vital game in Italy in November 1976, due to an epidemic of sore throats and colds which hit the squad.

That wasn't all to hit the line-up. Revie chose a completely new back line and a combative midfield designed to win the ball. But Trevor Brooking was the only player to do anything with the ball when won, and there was a lone front-runner in Stan Bowles (yes, I had to check it was him), so leaving out his previous two goalscorers Joe Royle and Stuart Pearson.

Italy had a formidable home record of only two defeats in 15 years. So Revie included a few choice Italian profanities in the dossiers he'd prepared for his team, to get them going. England managed to stifle Italy for half an hour but then the home side took a fortuitous lead when Antognoni's free kick was deflected past Clemence by Keegan.

Bettega's spectacular diving header with less than 15 minutes remaining confirmed victory. So, midway through the qualifying campaign, World Cup elimination loomed for England.

Luxembourg, like San Marino, is a nation more noted for its philatelic exports than its footballers and so when England faced the Duchy's finest, in the spring of 1977, hopes were high for a goal fest. All England had to do was run in a bucketful of goals in the two games before beating Italy, the former more achievable than the latter, maybe. Finland had already scored seven against Luxembourg, after all.

THE MANAGER: DON REVIE

Before the 1978 World Cup qualification began Revie refused to reveal his first team. He awarded 11 new caps in two consecutive games at the start of 1976. Of that number just Phil Neal and Mick Mills went on to develop meaningful international careers. While England were preparing in South America for a triple-header against Argentina, Brazil and Uruguay, Revie secretly met a United Arab Emirates delegation in Helsinki to discuss his managing the UAE team. The Football Association, blissfully unaware at the time, approached Revie about renewing his contract. Revie claimed he sought new employment because he thought the FA were about to sack him. In December 1978 an FA commission banned Revie from any involvement with English football for 10 years. A year on Revie had the ban overturned, but never worked in England again.

REVIE'S ENGLAND RECORD MARCH 1976 – JULY 1977

P	W	D	L	F	A	WIN %
19	8	5	6	27	18	42.1

THE MANAGER: RON GREENWOOD (1977)

After the sour experience of seeing the traitorous Revie desert the English World Cup '78 campaign in mid-sink, the FA reached out to Ron Greenwood. While in charge of West Ham Greenwood had nurtured the talents of the players who formed a large part of England's 1966 World Cup winning side – Moore, Hurst and Peters (he also took Jimmy Greaves to Upton Park after the tournament). It was hoped that his ability to develop young players combined with the respect given him by the older professionals in the squad would help create a miracle akin to that of the Hammers winning the FA Cup followed by the European Cup Winners Cup in 1964 and 1965. Unfortunately for everyone involved, Revie's legacy of confusion, distrust and bad results left Greenwood and England merely blowing bubbles back at home, watching the finals play out in Argentina on the telly.

England, decimated by injuries that robbed Revie of 10 players, gave a second cap to Trevor Francis, who scored two goals as did Mick Channon, with Ray Kennedy adding the other in a 5-0 win. In the seven months that passed before England went to Luxembourg for the return match, Don Revie skulked away to the United Arab Emirates, topping up his bank balance and tan but destroying his reputation. And so England appointed a new manager – Ron Greenwood. In June England's chances became decidedly dodgier after Italy beat Finland 3-0 and England had to score more than 5 in Luxembourg.

In only his second England game, and with goals the order of the day, the new England boss elected to play Emlyn Hughes as a sweeper, and give Ian Callaghan only his fourth (and final) cap 12 years after winning his first. England only managed to score twice, though, which meant that even if England beat Italy, the Italians would qualify as long as they beat Luxembourg. However, if England won by three goals at Wembley, the Azurri would need a three-goal winning margin against the Duchy.

Ron Greenwood selected three new caps to face Italy in November 1977, all attackers. Peter Barnes and Steve Coppell would provide the ammunition for Everton centre forward Bob Latchford. Trevor Francis

MOST DANGEROUS ENGLAND PLAYER

KEVIN KEEGAN. A busy, hardworking forward, who made up for a lack of natural ability with tremendous hard work. He scored four goals in the six World Cup qualifiers in which he played. Strangely, he only ever played for 26 minutes in one game in World Cup finals, in 1982.

MOST OVERRATED ENGLAND PLAYER

DON REVIE. Failure to reproduce club form on the international scene is not only a problem for players. Revie was the most successful club manager of his era, but in trying to replicate his methods on the international stage he failed miserably. Running away to the Middle East in the midst of trying to qualify cannot have been good for morale either.

was left on the bench. Keegan scored with a deflected header after just 10 minutes but there was never any danger of a goal torrent, although Barnes might have scored twice after England's opener.

To England's credit they turned on the style (so why not earlier in the campaign?), but a second goal didn't come until the 81st minute, through Brooking, and it wasn't enough. Italy duly beat Luxembourg 3-0, and England were eliminated on goal difference, the only nation to suffer that fate for that competition. Between them, Revie and Greenwood used 33 players in the six games, with only Clemence the ever-present.

When Revie left, only the Scots mourned: they'd beaten his side twice in a year, home and away.

THE 1978 WORLD CUP FINAL

Argentina 3 [Kempes (2), Bertoni] v Holland 1 [Naninga]
AET (1-1)
25 June 1978 (Buenos Aires)

WORLD CUP 1978 QUALIFYING

GROUP 2 WINNERS: ITALY

England 2nd P6/W5/D0/L1/F15/A4 did not qualify

Finland 1 [Paatelainen] v England 4 [Keegan (2), Channon, Pearson]
13 June 1976 (Helsinki)
Clemence, Todd, Mills, Thompson, Madeley, Cherry, Keegan, Channon, Pearson, Brooking, Francis G.

England 2 [Tueart, Royle] v Finland 1 [Nieminen]
13 Oct 1976 (Wembley)
Clemence, Todd, Beattie, Thompson, Greenhoff B, Wilkins, Keegan, Channon, Royle, *Brooking, **Tueart.
*Mills 75th min **Hill 75th min

Italy 2 [Antognoni, Bettega] v England 0
17 Nov 1976 (Rome)
Clemence, *Clement, Mills, Greenhoff, McFarland, Hughes, Keegan, Cherry, Channon, Bowles, Brooking.
*Beattie 75th min

England 5 [Channon (2, 1 pen) Kennedy, Francis T, Keegan] v Luxembourg 0
30 March 1977 (Wembley)
Clemence, Gidman, Cherry, Kennedy, Watson, Hughes, Keegan, Channon, *Royle, Francis T, Hill.
*Mariner 45th min

Luxembourg 0 v England 2 [Kennedy, Mariner]
12 October 1977 (Luxembourg City)
Clemence, Cherry, Hughes, *McDermott, **Watson, Kennedy, Wilkins, Francis T, Mariner, Hill, Callaghan.
*Whymark 65th min **Beattie 69th min

England 2 [Keegan, Brooking] v Italy 0
17 November 1977 (Wembley)
Clemence, Neal, Cherry, Wilkins, Watson, Hughes, *Keegan, Coppell, **Latchford, Brooking, Barnes P.
*Francis T 83rd min, **Pearson 75th min

ONE CAP WONDERS

Apart from Trevor Whymark, all of these players won medals and trophies during their club career, which is why they're my One Cap Wonders. None of them were picked by Sven, who tried to give every English player in the Premiership a cap during his time as England manager. They all (except Sutton and sub Marwood) got more minutes in an England shirt than Kevin Hector though, who wore it for 21 minutes over two games in 1973.

JOHN GIDMAN
(90 MINS, v LUXEMBURG 30/3/77, A WC QUALIFIER WIN 5-0)
Aston Villa ('71–'79), Everton ('79–'81), Man United ('81–'86), Manchester City ('86–'88), Stoke City ('88), Darlington ('88). An overlapping right back with an eye for goal, played 433 games (19 goals), in a 17-year career. Won the FA Cup with Man Utd. Picked by Don Revie.

TOMMY SMITH
(90 MINS, v WALES 19/5/71, HOME INT 0-0)
Liverpool ('62–'78), Swansea ('78–'79)
Centre back. Played 637 games for Liverpool (48 goals). Won five League Championships, two FA Cups and the UEFA Cups, twice at Anfield. Scored twice in 36 league games for Swansea before retiring. Picked by Alf Ramsey.

DANNY WALLACE
(90 MINS, v EGYPT 29/1/86, FRIENDLY WIN 0-4, 1 GOAL)
Saints ('80–'89), Man Utd ('89–'93) Birmingham ('93–'95)
Not many players score on a debut and do not play again for England. Scored 79 goals in 317 games for Saints, won the FA and European Cup Winners' Cups with Man Utd. Diagnosed with MS in 1996 and retired. Picked by Bobby Robson.

JOHN HOLLINS
(90 MINS, v SPAIN 24/5/67, FRIENDLY WIN 2-0)
Chelsea ('63–'75, '83–'84), QPR ('75–'79), Arsenal ('79–'83)
A hard-tackling midfielder, retired in 1984 after 939 senior games. Won the FA Cup, the Football League Cup and the European Cup Winners' Cup as well as being a runner-up in each at Arsenal. Picked by Alf Ramsey.

SUBS
GK Nigel Spink (45 mins, v Australia 19/6/83, Friendly 1-1)
Tony Brown (72 mins, v Wales 19/5/71, Home Int 0-0)
Neil Ruddock (90 mins, v Nigeria 16/11/94, Friendly win 1-0)
Mark Walters (70 mins, v New Zealand 3/6/91, Friendly win 1-0)
Brian Marwood (10 mins, v Saudi Arabia 16/11/88, Friendly 1-1)

CHARLIE GEORGE
(65 MINS, v REP. IRELAND 8/9/76, FRIENDLY 1-1)
Arsenal ('68–'75), Derby County ('75–'78, '82), Saints ('78–'81), Bulova HK ('81–'82), Bournemouth ('82) Dundee Utd ('82–'83)
Picked for England five years after scoring the goal that won Arsenal the Double and a year after a hat-trick against Real Madrid for Derby. Substituted. Picked by Don Revie.

GK: JIMMY RIMMER
(PLAYED FIRST 45 MINS, v ITALY 28/5/76, FRIENDLY WIN 3-2)
Man United ('65–'74), Swansea ('73 on loan), (Arsenal '74–'77), Aston Villa ('77–'83), Swansea ('83–'86)

Won two European Cup winners' medals, with Man Utd in 1968 as a sub, and after playing only eight minutes for Aston Villa in 1982 (due to a neck injury). Picked by Don Revie.

DAVID UNSWORTH
(90 MINS, v JAPAN 3/6/95, UMBRO INT TOURNAMENT WIN 3-1)
Everton ('91–'97, '98–'04), West Ham ('97–'98), Villa ('98), Portsm'th ('04–'05), Sheff Utd ('05–'07), Wigan ('07–)

A tough centre back with a long career in the Premiership. 116 league games in first Everton spell, 188 in second. Still in the Premiership at time of writing. Picked by Terry Venables.

NICHOLAS PICKERING
(90 MINS, v AUSTRALIA 19/6/83, FRIENDLY 1-1)
Sunderland ('81–'86), Coventry ('86–'87) Derby County ('88–'91), Darlington ('91–'92), Burnley ('93)

Left back. Scored 18 goals in 209 games for Sunderland, nine in 78 for Coventry (also won the FA Cup), three in 45 for Derby, seven in 57 for Darlington. Picked by Bobby Robson.

COLIN HARVEY
(90 MINS, v MALTA 3/2/71, WC QUALIFIER WIN 0-1)
Everton ('63–'75), Sheff Wednesday ('74–'76)

Scored 24 goals in 384 games from midfield for Everton, two in 48 for Wednesday. Won the FA Cup in 1966 and 1970 First Division Championship with Everton, playing alongside Alan Ball and Howard Kendall. Picked by Alf Ramsey.

TREVOR WHYMARK
(25 MINS, v LUXEMBURG 12/10/77, WC QUALIFIER WIN 0-2)
Ipswich ('69–'79), Derby County ('79), Grimsby ('80–'84), Southend ('84–'85), Peterborough ('85), Colchester ('85)

Scored 75 goals for Ipswich in 261 games, including four years in the UEFA Cup. Came on as a sub for Terry McDermott with England leading only 1-0. Picked by Ron Greenwood.

CHRIS SUTTON
(11 MINS, v CAMEROON 15/11/97, FRIENDLY WIN 2-0)
Norwich ('91–'94), Blackburn Rovers ('94–'99), Chelsea ('99–'00), Celtic ('00–'06), Birmingham City ('06), Aston Villa ('06–)

Won a Premiership with Blackburn, 3 SPL titles, the FSA and League Cups twice at Celtic. Cost £21 million in transfer fees. Refused an England B squad call-up. Picked by Glenn Hoddle.

MANAGER: PETER TAYLOR
(90 MINS, v ITALY 15/11/00, FRIENDLY, LOST 1-0)

The only manager to take charge of England for one game, he put 16 players on the pitch in Turin and made David Beckham captain for the first time. Managed England Under 21 side twice, from 1996–'99 and 2004–'07, getting them to the European Championships finals in June 2007. Managed Leicester City in the Premiership 2000–'01. They were relegated, he was sacked. Manager Crystal Palace 2006– .

MOST DANGEROUS ENGLAND PLAYER

JACK CHARLTON. He'd won the World Cup more than twenty years earlier; he'd won League titles and FA Cups with Leeds Utd. And now as a manager he took a tiny nation into a major competition and got them to a better finishing spot than England managed. He also uncovered a wealth of neglected talent in the English game, best epitomised by Ray Houghton, and made them internationals of quality.

MOST DANGEROUS OPPONENT

MARCO VAN BASTEN, who showed England how football should be played and went on to help Holland deservedly win the tournament by beating USSR. Van Basten scored the winner in the final with a volley that is widely considered one of the best goals ever. He ended the competition as top scorer, with five – three more than the next highest scorers and four more than the highest-scoring Englishmen, Bryan Robson and Tony Adams. He was European Player of The Year in 1988 (and 1989, and 1992 when he was also voted World Player of the Year). In a cruelly short career he scored 118 goals in 280 games at club level and 24 in 58 for Holland.

MOST OVERRATED ENGLISH PLAYER

GLENN HODDLE was an irritating combination of sublime skill and inconsistency of performance at international level. So much so that his England manager, Bobby Robson, wondered publicly at one point 'if he was a luxury, whether we can afford to play him'. Years later Robson didn't include him in his Dream Team selection for his autobiography and kept silent on what he thought of Hoddle's use of a psychic healer at England camps.

EUROPEAN CHAMPIONSHIPS 1988 QUALIFYING

GROUP 4 WINNERS: ENGLAND

England P6/W5/D1/L0/F19/A1

England 3 [Lineker (2) Waddle] v N. Ireland 0

15 Oct 1986 (Wembley)

England 2 [Anderson, Mabbutt] v Yugoslavia 0

12 Nov 1986 (Wembley)

N. Ireland 0 v England 2 [Robson, Waddle]

29 April 1987 (Belfast)

Turkey 0 v England 0

29 April 1987 (Izmir)

England 8 [Lineker (3) Barnes (2) Robson, Beardsley, Webb] v Turkey 0

14 Oct 1987 (Wembley)

Yugoslavia 1 [Katanec] v England 4 [Beardsley, Barnes, Robson, Adams]

11 Nov 1987 (Belgrade)

EUROPEAN CHAMPIONSHIPS 1988 FINALS

GROUP B WINNERS: USSR

England 4th P3/W0/D0/L3/F2/A7 (eliminated)

England 0 v Rep Ireland 1 [Houghton]

12 June 1988 (Stuttgart)

England 1 [Robson] v Holland 3 [Van Basten (3)]

15 June 1988 (Dusseldorf)

England 1 [Adams] v USSR 3 [Aleinikov, Pasulko, Mikhailichenko]

18 June 1988 (Frankfurt)

THE FINAL

USSR 0 v 2 Holland [Gullit, Van Basten]

25 June 1988 (Munich)

WORLD CUP ITALY 1990

'TEARS WE GO...' [THE *SUN*]

As one of the losing quarter-finalists in the 1986 World Cup, England hoped for, and became, a seeded team for Italia '90. They did so at the expense of Spain, the other nation in contention for the last favoured slot. Despite having the better finals record, English fans swung it for our boys – security considerations won the day – and England were shuttled away to Sardinia.

Fate conspired to group England with two teams that had beaten them in the 1988 Euro Championships, Ireland and Holland. With the fanatical Dutch fans regarded as even worse than English hooligans, UEFA and the British government braced itself for any backlash against trouble that could lead to a reversal of the governing body's decision to readmit English clubs to European competition the following year.

The fact that England had gone through the qualifying group unbeaten, without conceding a goal, generated optimistic home support. However, the squad itself was bereft of any truly world-class players except Gary Lineker and Bryan Robson. There was also Paul Gascoigne of course. Possessed of great natural talent 'Gazza' was a loose cannon who could transform any game in a twinkle but, equally quickly, could lose the ball – and the plot – in important positions.

The 1990 squad was by far the most experienced ever going into a World Cup, and Peter Shilton's 117 caps contributed greatly to that experience. Losing Robson in only the second game was a big blow.

'HAVE YOU EVER WITNESSED A MORE EMBARRASSING EXHIBITION OF WASTED ENERGY?' [*DAILY MAIL*]

The opening game with the Republic of Ireland was a typically British affair, with the ball spending most of the game in the air. Post-match stats show the ball in play for only 47 of the 90 minutes.

Lineker scored after eight minutes to match

Gazza cries his way home after a semi-final defeat

Hurst's achievement of scoring the last goal in a previous World Cup and the first in the next for England. The next 65 minutes of the game against the Irish was a bruising battle before a mistake by substitute Steve McMahon gifted Kevin Sheedy his equaliser.

For the Holland game, England manager Bobby Robson changed his formation to employ a sweeper for the first time in his eight-year tenure, with Mark

ENGLAND SQUAD

	CLUB	AGE	CAPS	GOALS
GOALKEEPERS				
Peter Shilton	Derby	40	117	
Chris Woods	Rangers	30	16	
David Seaman*	Arsenal	26	3	
Dave Beasant	Chelsea	31	2	
FULL BACKS				
Tony Dorigo	Cheslea	24	3	
Paul Parker	QPR	26	5	
Stuart Pearce	Notts Forest	28	23	1
Gary M Stevens	Rangers	27	38	
CENTRE BACKS				
Terry Butcher	Rangers	31	71	3
Des Walker	Notts Forest	24	17	
Mark Wright	Derby	26	23	
MIDFIELDERS				
Paul Gascoigne	Tottenham	22	10	2
Steve Hodge	Notts Forest	27	21	
Steve McMahon	Liverpool	28	12	
David Platt	Aston Villa	23	4	
Bryan Robson	Man Utd	33	84	26
Trevor Steven	Rangers	26	26	4
Neil Webb	Man Utd	26	19	2
FORWARDS				
John Barnes	Liverpool	26	52	10
Peter Beardsley	Liverpool	29	39	7
Steve Bull	Wolves	25	6	4
Gary Lineker	Tottenham	29	50	31
Chris Waddle	Marseilles	29	51	6

*After arriving in Italy David Seaman was injured in training and Dave Beasant replaced him

Previous page: BACK L-R: Waddle, Webb, Wright, Woods, Shilton, Seaman, Beasant, Steven T, Lineker, Bull, Pearce, Barnes, Butcher. FRONT L-R: Walker, Platt, McMahon, Dorigo, Parker, Stevens G, Beardsley, Gascoigne, Hodge. Robson B is missing, through injury

THE MANAGER: BOBBY ROBSON

Bobby had been a teammate of Johnny Haynes, England's first £100 a week footballer, at Fulham, before moving to West Brom where he excelled as an attacking midfielder. He won 20 England caps between 1958 and 1962 but never hit the heights of the game that he did as manager.

He returned to Craven Cottage to begin his coaching career under Ron Greenwood, and became Fulham manager in 1968 but was sacked after only nine months. He then became manager of Ipswich Town. After surviving an uncertain start to his tenure, he engineered a minor miracle and, on limited resources, turned the East Anglian club into a major football force, their success built on playing quality football on the ground.

In 1978 Ipswich won the FA Cup and at the start of the 1980s finished as First Division runners-up as well as claiming the 1981 UEFA Cup.

During his eight years in charge of England Robson took them to a World Cup quarter-final (in 1986) and a semi (in 1990), which was lost on penalties, making him the most successful England manager after Alf Ramsey. Forget about the European Championships in 1988, when England lost all three games (see page 95). He won almost half of the games that England played with him in charge, drew a third and lost only 18%.

Ultimately of course, Robson's reign will be best remembered for the team's success at Italia '90, their poorly taken penalties and what could and should have been only England's second World Cup final appearance.

ROBSON'S ENGLAND RECORD IN FULL

P	W	D	L	F	A	WIN %
95	47	30	18	154	60	49.47

WHY WAS HE THERE?

STEVE BULL had never played in the Second Division let alone the First, yet Robson made him the first player to be plucked from the Third Division since Peter Taylor in 1976. In his defence 'Bully' went to Italia '90 with a goals per game ratio bettered only by Gary Lineker.

WHY WASN'T HE THERE?

IAN WRIGHT twice broke his leg during the 1989–90 season but still scored two goals as a sub for Crystal Palace in the FA Cup Final against Man United. Despite setting a record of 27 league goals in 1989–90, he had to wait a year (and join Arsenal) before his debut.

Wright given the role. Dutch team selection wrecked that ploy and resulted in left-sided England centre half Terry Butcher playing at right back. Gascoigne dominated midfield and Des Walker had the edge over Dutch striker Marco van Basten, but the closest the match came to a goal was when England substitute Steve Bull flashed a header wide. A compelling game gave Peter Shilton a clean sheet to celebrate his world-record 120th cap and saw the elimination of Bryan Robson from the tournament with another crock; this time, fittingly, it was his Achilles heel that suffered.

Because all the group games had been draws England needed only a win over Egypt to clinch the group. And they had never lost to an African nation.

For the first time, for club or country, Robson dropped Butcher and captain Bryan Robson was unfit (despite a faith healer being flown out to aid his recuperation). England fielded a flat back four and Mark Wright, who replaced Terry Butcher, headed home the only goal of the game.

An uninspiring Second Round game with Belgium was one minute from penalties until David Platt's wonder volley, his first goal for England, set up a clash with Cameroon, the first African side to reach a World Cup quarter-final. The African team's over-physical approach had earned them two red and eight yellow cards and the suspension of four key players for the England match.

David Platt scored the 100th goal of Italia '90 to put England ahead but just past the hour Kunde and Ekeke earned Cameroon the lead. Back in London it was claimed that the celebrations in the Cameroon embassy were such that a terrorist raid was suspected and reported by neighbours.

Cameroon then attempted to sit back on their 2-1 lead rather than go for a third, of which they looked more than capable. But seven minutes from full time Lineker was felled in the box; he stood up, kept his nerve and converted England's first World Cup penalty for 20 years. In extra-time another Lineker spot kick earned England their first World Cup semi-final to be played on foreign soil.

'WE BEAT THEM IN '45, WE BEAT THEM IN '66, NOW THE BATTLE OF '90' [THE SUN]

England's opponents in the semi-final were the old enemy, West Germany. Since 1966 England had only beaten them twice in 10 attempts, and then both in friendly matches. England were in only their second semi-final; the Germans had reached the last four a total of eight times already.

A pulsating first half failed to create any clear-cut

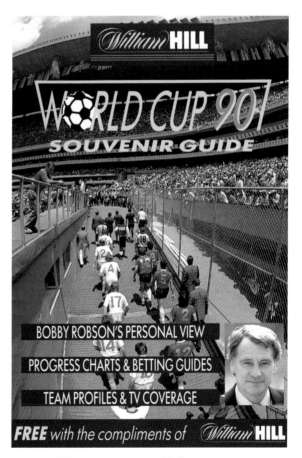

Who'd bet on England going out on penalties?

chances for either side but the Germans scored on the hour. A free kick was touched short to Brehme and his shot deflected off Parker and over Shilton. Once again Gary Lineker came to the rescue and scored his 10th World Cup goal, earning extra-time. Paul Gascoigne was later booked and realised that this, his second yellow card of the tournament, would mean that he had to miss the final. He broke down in tears on the pitch and produced the defining image of the tournament.

West Germany had dominated England in extra-time, but the English hit the post through Waddle. The

MOST DANGEROUS ENGLAND PLAYER

In 1990 there was no better goalscorer in the world than **GARY LINEKER**. Not only was he a supreme penalty box predator but his ability to keep a cool head while those around him lost theirs, as typified by his successful penalties against Cameroon, proved to be without equal. Lineker could disguise his intent when attempting to score, dummying keeper or defender or forcing them to make mistakes, which brought him 48 goals in 80 internationals. Only Bobby Charlton had scored (one) more, in 106 games.

game finished goalless and so it went to penalties.

Few supporters can remember who scored from the spot that day but everyone knows it was Pearce and Waddle who didn't. At least Psycho hit the target, with Illgner saving with his legs. Waddle's shot not only sailed over the bar, but it cleared the running track and ended up in the arms of a fan who went on to auction it on eBay, ten years later. That fan had been a hundred metres away from the spot that marked the end of yet another England World Cup dream.

England did at least return with something, though. Yes, they lost the new third place play-off game to hosts Italy 2-1, but they were awarded the FIFA Fair Play Trophy, for fewest red and yellow cards collected and fewest fouls committed.

MAP OF VENUES

Group **A** ROME/FLORENCE
Italy, Austria, USA, Czechoslovakia

Group **B** NAPLES/BARI
Argentina, Cameroon, USSR, Romania

Group **C** TURIN/GENOVA
Brazil, Sweden, Costa Rica, Scotland

Group **D** MILAN/BOLOGNA
W. Germany, Yugoslavia, UAE, Colombia

Group **E** VERONA/UDINE
Belgium, S. Korea, Uruguay, Spain

Group **F** CAGLIARI/PALERMO
England, Eire, Holland, Egypt

MATCH DATES

JUNE 11		
Group C	**COSTA RICA v SCOTLAND**	Genoa at 4.00pm BST
Group E	**ENGLAND v EIRE**	Cagliari at 8.00pm BST
JUNE 16		
Group C	**SWEDEN v SCOTLAND**	Genoa at 8.00pm BST
Group F	**ENGLAND v HOLLAND**	Cagliari at 8.00pm BST
JUNE 17		
Group F	**EIRE v EGYPT**	Palermo at 4.00pm BST
JUNE 20		
Group C	**BRAZIL v SCOTLAND**	Turin at 8.00pm BST
JUNE 21		
Group F	**ENGLAND v EGYPT**	Cagliari at 8.00pm BST
Group F	**EIRE V HOLLAND**	Palermo at 8.00pm BST

A very useful guide to who, where and when at Italia '90

WORLD CUP 1990 FINALS

GROUP F WINNERS: ENGLAND

England 1st P4/W1/D2/L0/F2/A1

England 1 (Lineker) v Republic of Ireland 1 (Sheedy)

11 June 1990 (Cagliari)

England 0 v Holland 0

16 June 1990 (Cagliari)

England 1 (Wright) v Egypt 0

21 June 1990 (Cagliari)

ROUND OF 16

England 1 (Platt) v Belgium 0 (AET)

26 June 1990 (Bologna)

QUARTER-FINAL

England 3 (Platt, Lineker 2 pens) v Cameroon 2 (Kunde, Ekeke) (AET)

1 July 1990 (Naples)

SEMI-FINAL

England 1 (Lineker) v West Germany 1 (Parker o.g.) (AET)

West Germany win 4-3 on penalties

4 July 1990 (Turin)

THIRD PLACE PLAY-OFF

England 1 (Platt) v Italy 2 (Baggio, Schillaci pen)

7 July 1990 (Bari)

THE FINAL

Argentina 0 v West Germany 1 (Brehme, pen)

8 July 1990 (Rome)

ENGLAND'S WORST EVER TEAM

There are so many candidates for this team, but the choice of captain encapsulates all that has been so wrong with the English national team. Carlton Palmer's career trophies number 0, but his transfer sums add up to £6 million. As manager of Stockport County he asked, 'Who is to say I won't be manager of England in 10 years time?' They were relegated after a record 32 defeats.

GLEN JOHNSON ('03–'05, CAPS 5)

West Ham ('01–'03), Chelsea ('03–), Portsmouth ('06–'07 loan)

After only 15 games for West Ham (and eight at Millwall on loan), was transferred to Chelsea for loads of dosh. Capped by Sven for two starts, got two yellow cards and impressed no-one in any of the friendlies he played. Loaned out by Chelsea and not recalled despite injury problems in 2006–7.

GRAHAM ROBERTS ('83–'84, CAPS 6)

Weymouth ('78–'80), Spurs ('80–'87), Rangers ('87–'88), Chelsea ('88–'90), WBA ('90–'92)

Won Cups with Spurs and Rangers. Games for England included just two wins (one v Scotland, one v N. Ireland), two draws (same opposition) and two losses, both friendlies (0-2 to France, 0-2 to USSR), all for Bobby Robson.

TONY TOWERS ('76, CAPS 3)

Man City ('69–'74), Sunderland ('74–'77), Birmingham ('77–'81)

Was a makeweight in the deal which took Dennis Tueart and Mick Horswill to Man City for £275,000 from Sunderland. Played for England against Wales (won 1-0), N. Ireland (on as a sub for 23 minutes in a 4-0 win) and Italy (a 3-2 win in the US Bicentennial Tournament, in New York). But why?

PAUL STEWART ('91–'92, CAPS 3)

Blackpool ('81–'87), Man City ('87–'88), Spurs ('88–'92), Liverpool ('92–'96), Crystal Palace ('94 loan), Wolves ('94 loan), Burnley ('95 loan), Sunderland ('95 loan, '96–'97), Stoke ('97–'98)

Total playing time for England 78 minutes, one loss (to Germany), two draws. Always confident of his own abilities, none of his 10 managers could see his true brilliance.

SUBS

GK Dave Beasant ('89, caps 2)
Broke his foot with a jar of mayonnaise, his nickname was Lurch.

Mike Duxbury ('83–'84, caps 10)
At Man Utd he won two FA Cups. Because he was at Man Utd.

Bob McNab ('68–'69, caps 4)
Now best known as the father of Mercedes McNab, a co-star of Buffy the Vampire Slayer.

Brian Deane ('91–'92, caps 3)
Scored seven goals in 18 games for Benfica, apparently.

GARRY BIRTLES ('80, CAPS 3)

Notts Forest ('76–'80, '82–'87), Man Utd ('80–'82), Notts County ('87–'88), Grimsby Town ('88–'91)

Cost Man Utd £1.25 million. Didn't score for England, but didn't finish a game, either. Played 15 mins as sub in a 3-1 friendly win against Argentina, 75 mins against Italy in 1-0 loss, and 65 mins in a 2-1 loss to the Czechs. Had a beard.

GK: RICHARD WRIGHT ('00–'01, CAPS 2)

Ipswich Town ('94–'01), Arsenal ('01–'02), Everton ('02–)

Cost Arsenal £6 million and played only 12 games (1 o.g.). At Everton, he fell out of his loft and in 2006 injured himself warming up. First cap in a 2-1 friendly win away to Malta, 2nd as half-time sub for Nigel Martyn in friendly loss to Holland at White Hart Lane. Been in 30 England squads.

STEVE FOSTER ('82, CAPS 3)

Portsmouth ('75–'79), Brighton & Hove Albion ('79–'84, '92–'96), Aston Villa ('84), Luton Town ('84–'89), Oxford Utd ('89–'92)

Famous for always wearing a fluffy white tennis headband, won the League Cup with Luton in 1989. England didn't concede in any of his three games, but they were against N. Ireland, Kuwait and Holland starring no-one you'd recall.

PAUL KONCHESKY ('03-'05, CAPS 2)

Charlton Athletic ('99–'05), West Ham ('05–)

Sven capped an enormous number of players, some of whom deserved a chance. Konchesky however, didn't. With Ashley Cole and Wayne Bridge as first-choice left backs Sven still tried him out for 45 mins against Australia (lost 1-3) and 45 v Argentina (won 3-2). Unlikely to ever gain another cap.

CARLTON PALMER ('92–'93, CAPS 18, 1 GOAL)

WBA ('84–'89), Sheff Wed ('89–'94, '01 loan), Leeds Utd ('94–'97), Saints ('97–'99), Notts Forest ('99), Coventry ('99–'01), Watford ('00–'01 loan), Stockport County ('01–'03), Mansfield ('05)

Not a misprint. Carlton has 18 caps. And he scored in a World Cup qualifier (a 6-0 win over San Marino at Wembley). Often preferred to Steve Bruce. Why? Ask the turnip.

ERIC GATES ('80, CAPS 2)

Ipswich Town ('73–'85), Sunderland ('85–'90), Carlisle ('90–'91)

Under Bobby Robson at Ipswich Eric Lazenby Gates scored 96 goals in 345 games and won the 1978 FA Cup and the 1981 UEFA Cup. But it was Greenwood who gave him his two caps. Unfortunately, the second was only for the first half of a World Cup qualifier that England lost 2-1 in Bucharest.

JOHN FASHANU ('89, CAPS 2)

Norwich ('79–'83), Crystal Palace ('83 loan), Lincoln City ('83–'84), Millwall ('84–'86), Wimbledon ('86–'94), Aston Villa ('94)

Was involved in a match-fixing scandal and retired to work in TV (*Gladiators*) in 1995. Both caps came in a friendly tournament at Wembley. Played 71 mins in a 0-0 with Chile, and 31 mins in a 2-0 win over Scotland (replaced by Steve Bull).

MANAGER: HOWARD WILKINSON

Managed Notts County ('82–'83), Sheff Wed ('83–'88), Leeds Utd ('88–'96), Sunderland ('02–'03)

As a club manager he won the Second and First Division titles, both with Leeds and er, that's it. Took temporary charge of the England squad after the sacking of Glenn Hoddle and lost 2-0 to France. Took charge of the national team again after Keegan's departure, for a 0-0 with Finland. Managed Sunderland to their record run of 19 defeats in the Premiership and was sacked (they were relegated).

Wilkinson's England record: P2/W0/D1/L1/F0/A2

WORLD CUP JAPAN/KOREA 2002

'I WILL MAKE IT' [THE *DAILY EXPRESS*]

In 1970 we wuz robbed by a stolen bracelet and food poisoning. In 2002 we wuz robbed by a metatarsus – an English one at that.

The 2002 World Cup would be the eighth since Hurst's glorious hat-trick. After beating the Germans 5-1 in Munich during qualifying, the English media, with its usual restraint and level-headed analysis of England's chances of winning the trophy again, declared that, naturally, England would win it. Just as long as a certain metatarsal bone healed in time. That it belonged to Goldenballs, David Beckham (fractured during a Champions League game in which he played for Man Utd against Deportivo La Coruna), meant that it was front-page news everywhere. Even in medical journals. It wasn't only his either. His Old Trafford teammate (and best man at the Wedding of the Century © tabloids everywhere) Gary Neville also busted a pesky small bone in his foot before the competition, and he definitely wouldn't make it. No-one seemed to care too much about Gary's availability, except the rugged and uncompromising Danny Mills, a shaven-headed Englishman who would have had 'Made in England' tatooed on his forehead if he thought that it would get him a game for England at right back. As it turned out he didn't need to, since for some reason Sven the Manager decided that Mills would replace Neville.

Ever the PR man, Sven knew that he had no replacement for his captain and People's Favourite. Four years later Sven would include two players in a World Cup squad because he thought the tabloids would crucify him if he didn't. He set the precedent for that here. Beckham would never say no to a game and despite not being fully fit, travelled to the Land of the Rising Yen-for-Replica-Shirts.

Sadly for Liverpudlians, Steven Gerrard injured his groin in Liverpool's final Premiership game of the 2001/2002 season, and since the press were busy

The full England squad pose on the steps of their transport to Japan and Korea. Danny Murphy (4th from bottom) broke a metatarsal in training and returned home.

ENGLAND SQUAD

	CLUB	AGE	CAPS	GOALS
GOALKEEPERS				
David Seaman	Arsenal	38	68	
David James	West Ham	32	9	
Nigel Martyn	Leeds	35	23	
FULL BACKS				
Danny Mills	Leeds	25	7	
Ashley Cole	Arsenal	21	8	
Wayne Bridge	S'hampton	21	5	
CENTRE BACKS				
Rio Ferdinand	Leeds	23	22	
Gareth Southgate	Middlesbro'	31	49	1
Sol Campbell	Arsenal	27	46	
Wes Brown	Man Utd	23	6	
Martin Keown	Arsenal	35	43	
MIDFIELDERS				
David Beckham	Man Utd	27	49	6
Paul Scholes	Man Utd	27	44	13
Kieron Dyer	Newcastle	23	9	
Nicky Butt	Man Utd	27	18	
Owen Hargreaves	B Munich	21	6	
Joe Cole	West Ham	21	6	
Trevor Sinclair	West Ham	29	5	
FORWARDS				
Michael Owen	Liverpool	22	36	16
Emile Heskey	Liverpool	24	24	3
Teddy Sheringham	Tottenham	36	47	11
Robbie Fowler	Leeds	27	25	7

Previous page: BACK L-R: Owen, Campbell, Heskey, Mills, Seaman, Ferdinand. FRONT L-R: Butt, Cole, Beckham, Scholes, Sinclair line up before the game against Denmark, which they won 3-0.

THE MANAGER: SVEN GORAN ERIKSSON

When Sven Goran Eriksson was announced as the first foreign England manager, Jack Charlton said it was 'a terrible mistake', while PFA chief executive Gordon Taylor commented, 'It is a very sad day for English football and a terrible indictment of our national association.' However, as one wag in the national press put it, we'd had a turnip as a manager, so why not try a Swede as well?

Sven had been a right back in the Swedish Second Division until forced to retire through injury. He started his coaching career with Swedish Third Division club Degerfors before graduating to Gothenburg, where he won the 1981 League Championship and the 1982 UEFA Cup. Over the next 18 years he won the League Championships of Portugal and Italy, along with another 11 club trophies.

He set about ensuring qualification for the 2002 World Cup, with success. However, the press noted that he didn't know whether 4-4-2 or a 'diamond' formation suited England best. Nor did he pick players who could adapt to a change of tactics within a game. He also chose to play in-form players out of position.

Yet he did make the quarter-finals of the 2002 World Cup after only seven months in charge. However, it was reported that an England player who had been in the squad in Japan and Korea said of Sven's half-time talks that, 'when things were going wrong the players needed Winston Churchill – but we got Iain Duncan Smith.'

SVEN'S ENGLAND RECORD 28 FEB 2001 – 21 JUNE 2002

P	W	D	L	F	A	WIN %
20	10	7	3	33	14	50

DANNY MILLS was the main beneficiary of Gary Neville's absence in Japan and Korea, since for some strange reason he was chosen as the Mancunian's replacement at full back. He was uncompromising in the way that so endears a player to the thug element among fans, but Mills was an average, no-frills English defender who couldn't cross a road, let alone provide a service for strikers.

GARETH BARRY had already been capped six times at full international level. He was and remains among the best in the position of left wing-back. He could tackle like a left back, create like a midfielder and cross like a left winger. Throw in his versatility at centre back and the fact that he was likely to pop up with a goal, and you have five good reasons to question why Sven didn't take him East.

looking left, Sven felt comfortable enough to not include a crocked Gerrard in his squad.

Sports writers in England concerned themselves with filling England's left side of midfield. The absence of a natural wing-back polarised opinion between those who would select a player who was left footed and those who'd choose a right-footed player who could come inside and shoot or pass (such as Joe Cole) but would not produce crosses from that flank. Cole played on the left in the last friendly game before the finals, against

Cameroon, and so was apparently Sven's choice for the position at the World Cup.

'THE GROUP OF DEATH' (THE *SUN*)

When the tournament began England's first game in the 'Group of Death' was against Sweden. The metatarsal bone lasted an hour before being replaced by Kieron Dyer. Sven might as well have replaced Beckham with a training cone. With England leading courtesy of goalscoring machine Sol Campbell (first goal in 46

EMILE HESKEY. Never punched his significant weight, at either club or international level. Perhaps he felt inhibited about using his ample physique in his role as a striker for fear of being punished by referees. He could have been an England regular for years – and it seemed as if he would, much to everyone but his own despair – but when it was finally pointed out that he had 'striker' in his job description and that they were expected to score goals, he was finally dropped. After winning the last of his 43 caps against France in 2004 his goal tally for England stood at five.

games), Danny Mills took it upon himself to give the Swedes a chance. His chest pass failed to reach goalkeeper Seaman and Alexandersson nipped in to level the scores. England then began to give the ball away regularly and lose their shape, but still managed a draw. In the second game of the group phase, England fought Argentina and miraculously won thanks to a penalty scored by the recovering metatarsal bone.

England won qualification with a dull goalless draw against Nigeria and set up a Second Round meeting with Denmark. Which was a stroke of luck, since the Danes decided that England needed to score a few goals in order to wind up English fans into a fever of optimism. Denmark let Owen, Ferdinand and even Emile Heskey score to earn a quarter-final against Brazil. Win this one, went English thinking, and we've won the Cup. Which goes to show how tenuous the grasp on reality was for English sports writers, fans and even players. They'd forgotten that you only won after contesting the actual final, but who could remember what that was like?

After the quarter-final, England blamed the heat (no food poisoning, though) for their inability to beat Brazil, who played the last half hour with 10 men. Michael Owen put England ahead midway through the first half, but 10 minutes of madness either side of the

MOST DANGEROUS OPPONENT

RONALDINHO masterminded Brazil's victory over England and was also behind his team's ultimate success in the final of the 2002 World Cup. Despite his dubious hairstyle and ever-present grin, it was obvious that here was a truly gifted, unique footballing talent. Not only did the ball stick to him, but it seemed to be mesmerised by his step-overs, feints and balletic moves. He looked thin but was substantial enough to ride tackles and even knock opponents off the ball. His like had never been seen in a World Cup. Pelé was stocky and physically different, as was Maradona. Only George Best could really have been compared with Ronaldinho. Big Phil Scolari, the Brazil manager and Bruce Forsyth fan (far left), turned down the chance to manage England after Sven had been pensioned off.

MOST DANGEROUS ENGLAND PLAYER

MICHAEL OWEN. Even though below par, he still managed to be the only England player to score more than one goal. Opposition teams identified him as the chief English goal threat and despite trying to mark him out of games, Owen's speed and agility ensured that he'd always get a couple of real chances in any match. That is, as long as his teammates could pass the ball to him and not the opposition, which sadly wasn't always the case.

interval did for Sven's men. David Beckham, on orders from his metatarsal bone, pulled out of a touchline challenge between a couple of Brazilians. The ball broke to Ronaldinho, who fed Rivaldo and he equalised. It was 1-1 at the break.

Five minutes into the second half Brazil were awarded a free-kick 45 yards from England's goal on the left touchline. Only Ronaldinho knows if he meant to float the free-kick over 'Safe Hands' in the England goal. He said afterwards that of course he intended to score. The ball caught Seaman too far off his line and

WORLD CUP 2002 QUALIFYING
GROUP 9 WINNERS: ENGLAND
England P8/W5/D2/L1/F16/A6 (Germany 2nd)
England 0 v Germany 1 [Hamann]
7 Oct 2000 (Wembley)
Finland 0 v England 0
11 Oct 2000 (Helsinki)
England 2 [Owen, Beckham] v Finland 1 [Riihilahti]
24 Mar 2001 (Liverpool)
Albania 1 [Rraklli] v England 3 [Owen, Scholes, Cole]
28 Mar 2001 (Tirane)
Greece 0 v England 2 [Scholes, Beckham]
6 June 2001 (Athens)
Germany 1 [Jancker] v England 5 [Owen 3, Gerrard, Heskey]
1 Sept 2001 (Munich)
England 2 [Owen, Fowler] v Albania 0
5 Sept 2001 (Newcastle)
England 2 [Sheringham, Beckham] v Greece 2 [Charisteas, Nikolaidis]
6 Oct 2001 (Manchester)

WORLD CUP 2002 FINALS
GROUP F WINNERS: SWEDEN
England 2nd: P3/W1/D2/L0/F2/A1
England 1 [Campbell] v Sweden 1 [Alexandersson]
2 June 2002 (Siatama)
Argentina 0 v England 1 [Beckham, pen]
7 June 2002 (Sapporo)
Nigeria 0 v England 0
12 June 2002 (Osaka)
THE ROUND OF 16
Denmark 0 v England 3 [Ferdinand, Owen, Heskey]
15 June 2002 (Niigata)
QUARTER-FINAL
England [Owen] 1 v Brazil 2 [Rivaldo, Ronaldinho]
21 June 2002 (Fukuroi)
THE FINAL
Brazil 2 [Ronaldo, 2] v 0 West Germany
30 June 2002 (Yokohama)

with that ridiculous ponytail flapping desperately behind him, he tried to back-peddle on realising that the ball was dropping over him, and under the bar.

Seven minutes later the sublime Ronaldinho was adjudged to have fouled Danny Mills (which was patently ridiculous) and was sent off for a second yellow card.

As if accepting the natural order of football, England then let Brazil stroll to their victory. Owen faded after his goal, Beckham's metatarsus twinged, Seaman proved closer to a career as a ballroom dancer than he'd let on and no-one could rescue England.

It's rumoured that the metatarsal bone auditioned for a couple of roles in Hollywood films after the World Cup, but they eventually went to Beckham's old foe Vinny Jones, instead. At least we beat the Germans 5-1 in Munich in qualifying. Did I mention that?

WHERE'S GEOFF?

By now Sir Geoff Hurst was promoting the paperback edition of his best-selling autobiography, *1966 And All That*. Sir Geoff had written a new chapter all about how he hoped Beckham and Owen would be collecting the World Cup at the end of the tournament. He was, he wrote, retiring from the limelight now. Sir Geoff still worked promoting various companies within the game, though, and was happy to be – if asked – part of any new English bid to host a future World Cup.

EUROPEAN CHAMPIONSHIPS PORTUGAL 2004

'ERIKSSON'S TINKERING CANNOT DISGUISE LACK OF WINNING' (THE *INDEPENDENT*)

England made it to Euro 2004 with Goldenballs wearing the captain's armband. Wayne Rooney's emergence as a raw but exciting goalscorer in the Premiership during 2002 was useful for Sven and England, too.

Other new faces in the England team appeared in their thousands during a seemingly endless round of friendlies that were played between qualifying games. Alan Smith, a striker who could also play in midfield, debuted and scored against Portugal in 2002. Jonathan Woodgate, Smith's Leeds teammate, and Canadian Owen Hargreaves (of Bayern Munich) also made their first appearances for the team.

Yet the first team almost picked itself at this time. In front of first-choice goalkeeper David James was a solid, if occasionally nervous, centre half pairing of John Terry and Rio Ferdinand, with Gary Neville and Ashley Cole either side. A four-man midfield of Steven Gerrard, David Beckham and Paul Scholes, plus AN Other, on the left was the supply line to the developing strike pair of Owen and Rooney. That left midfield slot proved to be something of a long-running problem, and although Joe Cole eventually won the struggle with Ledley King for the position, he was a right-footed player.

Another problem for England was the lack of goalscoring cover for Rooney and Owen. Jermaine Defoe missed out on the trip to Portugal in favour of Darius Vassell, who always performed better for the national team than he did for his club, Aston Villa. Sven was later to admit his error in omitting Defoe.

However, if the newspapers were to be believed (and who wouldn't?) Sven's build-up to Portugal was being compromised by the possibility of his joining Chelsea as manager. In order to focus their manager's mind on the job in hand, the Football Association decided that, instead of reminding Sven of his contractual obligations, they should extend his tenure

Sven and Mark Pallios meet some stewardesses on the way to Portugal

on improved terms. These were that he would be paid excessive amounts of money AFTER he left the job, which was to be after the 2006 World Cup.

'SVEN WILL WE EVER LEARN?' (*SUNDAY MIRROR*)

Euro 2004 kicked off with England losing to France, with Beckham missing a penalty. Wayne Rooney dominated the necessary win over Switzerland that came five days later, adding two goals to one by Gerrard. He repeated his brace against Croatia with Scholes and Lampard also scoring, but Croatia also scored two. In the quarter-final England faced the host nation and after 27